Both Feet in One Shoe

My Story of Leaving Italy and and Making a New Life in San Francisco

By Rose Rinaldi
With Patricia Lynn Henley

Copyright © 2016 Rose Rinaldi.

All rights reserved. No part of this book may be reproduced, stored, or transmitted by any means—whether auditory, graphic, mechanical, or electronic—without written permission of both publisher and author, except in the case of brief excerpts used in critical articles and reviews. Unauthorized reproduction of any part of this work is illegal and is punishable by law.

ISBN: 978-1-4834-5755-0 (sc)
ISBN: 978-1-4834-5754-3 (e)

Because of the dynamic nature of the Internet, any web addresses or links contained in this book may have changed since publication and may no longer be valid. The views expressed in this work are solely those of the author and do not necessarily reflect the views of the publisher, and the publisher hereby disclaims any responsibility for them.

Any people depicted in stock imagery provided by Thinkstock are models, and such images are being used for illustrative purposes only.
Certain stock imagery © Thinkstock.

Lulu Publishing Services rev. date: 09/07/2016

*To our parents,
who gave us so much,
and to all the wonderful people
who helped me when
I needed help.*

Rose, age 2

Chapter 1

Coming to the United States from Italy when I was 12 years old was not easy. I stayed with a series of wonderful people who did not even know me before I got here. Each time, I met them when I moved in with them. Each time, they took me in and took care of me. For that I am grateful to all of them. But it was not easy. It was not unpleasant, but it was not easy.

I came here in 1953 with my loving Papa, may he rest in peace. My 15-year-old brother Pietro had come to San Francisco the year before, on his own, so he was waiting for us when my Papa and I arrived in June 1953. My Papa was actually born in the United States, in New York City, but his family moved back to Italy when he was four years old. His Mama suffered from emphysema.

April 30, 1953: Pete, Rose and Papa

The doctor told my Nonno, "If you want wealth, if you want a job, stay here. But if you want your wife, go back to Italy."

So in 1907 my Nonno took his wife and three sons back to Italy, to his hometown, a little place called Verbicaro, in the Calabria region in the south of Italy. That is where my Papa grew up, married my Mama, and raised my older brother, my younger sister, and me.

In the 1950s, U.S. immigration laws changed: a person who had been born in the United Stated but was now a citizen of another country could get a U.S. passport for one son or daughter who was less than 18 years old. That is how my 14-year-old brother Pietro came to San Francisco alone in 1952. The law changed again in 1953, and my Papa and I were able to get U.S. passports. My Mama and my younger sister, Carmela, had to stay behind in Italy.

For the year that my brother Pietro lived in San Francisco by himself, he stayed with one of my Mama's first cousins, and her family. Just before my Papa and I were due to arrive in San Francisco, that family came back to Italy for a long visit. Now 15 years old and called Peter instead of Pietro, my brother needed some place to stay while he waited for us to arrive. So he moved in with a family friend, Olga, her husband Gigu, and their son. They were renting a two-bedroom flat on Chestnut Street. Olga and her husband Gigu slept in one bedroom, and their son had the other bedroom with his Nonna. (They would soon have company, because Olga was expecting.) There was also a tiny little room by the front door. There was just enough space for a single bed, and that is where my brother stayed for the few weeks until Papa and I arrived. It is also where I eventually slept when I arrived in San Francisco.

Once we were here, Peter and Papa moved into a two-bedroom flat on Valencia Street, in the Mission district. A young man from Italy who was a friend of Gigu's was living in one of the bedrooms. My Papa and Peter moved into the other bedroom, and split the rent with the young man, but there was no place for me in that flat. We could not afford a larger place, with room for me. Plus, Peter and my Papa were almost never home. My Papa was out looking for work all day long, and when he found a job he worked six days a week. When my brother Peter was not in school, he sold newspapers at the corner of Polk and Broadway. So it was not a good place for a little girl to live.

Instead, I moved into the room where Peter had been staying with Olga and her husband Gigu, and their two boys. My room was not much bigger than the twin bed that was in it, but I liked it because it gave me a bit of privacy, with a door and everything. The room also had a small window, and at times I could hear people going up and down the stairs to the upstairs unit, where the owners of the building lived.

When I first moved in, Olga and Gigu only had one son, with another baby due soon. About a week later, I was at church with Olga's Mama when Gigu came hurrying to get us. Olga was in labor. She gave birth to their second baby boy. Of course, I did everything I could to help with the baby, and with the older boy.

I was 12 years old, and I think at that age you still need your Mama, but my Mama and younger sister were in Italy. I saw my Papa and brother once a week, on Sundays, so in many ways I was pretty much on my own. I was a good kid, and I did my best not to be a burden. I did my chores, I helped with the children and I was happy.

Gigu was Sicilian, and a very nice man. He worked in a restaurant down in North Beach, and he was an incredible cook. One time while I was there, they invited a lot of people over for dinner, maybe 8 to 12 people, I do not remember for sure. He cooked a beautiful meal, just wonderful, with a huge platter of fish, and lots of other dishes. We had a great time.

But after everybody left, I thought to myself, *Oh no, there is so much to clean up. All those dishes.*

"We have had a long day," Gigu told me. "We will leave everything in the sink, and tomorrow, we will do the dishes, you and I."

Well, still to this day, if I have anything in my mind, I have got to do it. Otherwise, I cannot sleep.

I went to bed, and I fell asleep. I did not know it, but I got up in the middle of the night and started sleepwalking. I did all the dishes. I cleaned up the entire place. I think the noise I made woke up Gigu. He saw what I was doing and realized that I was sleepwalking. He watched me, to make sure I did not hurt myself. Finally I went back to bed, without ever waking up. I had no idea what I had done.

When I got up in the morning and saw that everything was clean, I felt terrible. I thought Gigu had done it, even though he had told me we would wait until morning. I was upset.

"Don't worry," Gigu told me. "It is okay. I couldn't sleep, I had a few drinks, and the baby kept crying a little bit, so I cleaned. Don't worry, it is fine."

A few weeks later, Gigu and Olga got a chance to move to another place. It was a good deal for them, but there was no room for me. Before they left, Gigu told me that I had been sleepwalking the night of the big dinner, and I was the one who cleaned up the house.

"I was watching you, because you never know if something bad could happen to a person when they sleepwalk," he told me. "I did not want to startle you, so I just watched, and made sure you were safe."

Well, that was actually the second time I had sleepwalked. Once, back in Italy, my Mama took me to visit a shrine on a mountaintop, about a three- or four-hour walk from our home. As we were coming back it got kind of late, and we had to stop for the night about a half an hour walk from our town. There was a house being built in this village. It was not finished yet and was completely empty, but it had walls and a roof, so the people who owned it let a big group of us stay in it.

The place was full, with everyone sleeping on the floor. And me, I got up and started walking on the people, in my sleep. Everyone screamed, and I jerked awake. My Mama thought I was having a heart attack or something, but I was just sleepwalking. So I believed Gigu when he told me I cleaned the whole place by myself, in my sleep.

Since I could not live with Olga and her family any more, I moved in with one of Olga's sisters, Yolanda. She lived on Alemany Boulevard with her husband, their son, and their two daughters. Her husband's parents had a bedroom and kitchen downstairs. We lived upstairs, with Yolanda and her husband in one room, and the three children in a second bedroom. I stayed with the kids, on a roll-away bed that we folded in half and put in the closet each morning, and took out each night to make my bed. They were really nice to me, but I felt like I was in the way, so my Papa and I looked for another place where I could stay.

I moved in with Olga and Yolanda's third sister, Elvira, her husband and their family, in a place on Vienna Street. She was a hairdresser, and worked downstairs in a little room behind the garage. Again, it was a two-bedroom home. Elvira and Jim slept in one bedroom, and their young children had the other bedroom. I slept on a fold-out bed in the kids' room. The family was really nice to me. I liked living with them, and I stayed there for awhile, but then Elvira and her family had to move to San Jose, and I needed another place to stay.

My uncle Vincenzo and his daughter Carmela had also taken advantage of the change in immigration laws to come to San Francisco on U.S. passports, a little bit after my Papa and I came here. They rented a room in a garage in a house on Naples Street. It was a nice room, even though it was in the garage, and had a little kitchen. My uncle asked the landlord if I could live there too, and he said yes. So that was my fourth home in San Francisco in less than six months, living with my uncle Vincenzo and cousin Carmela.

It would have been a long, lonely bus ride for me to go to see my Papa and brother on Sundays, so instead they started coming to visit me, cousin Carmela, and Uncle Vincenzo. Carmela was a couple of years older than me, and we used to cook a little dinner, whatever we knew how to make. My Papa and brother would bring their laundry, and I would wash it for them. It made for a nice visit, and I liked the feeling of being a family, at least one day a week.

After two, maybe three weeks of this, the landlord told my cousin that I was using too much water, and I had to leave. My cousin and my uncle felt badly about this, but there was nothing they could do. The landlord would not change his mind. A few days later, on Sunday, I packed my little suitcase, and waited outside for my Papa to come pick me up.

As I waited, I was sad, and worried. I remember I kept thinking, just how much water did I use? I did not mean to do anything wrong. I just wanted to help my Papa and my brother. Now, I had to move. I was not sure where I was going to live next.

As they often did after church on Sundays, many of the neighbors were outside, sitting in chairs, talking and visiting. An older couple, Antonio and Mary Sarro, may they rest in peace, saw that I looked unhappy, and came over to talk with me. They were in their late 60s or early 70s. He worked in a shoeshine stand on Geneva Street. She had cataracts, poor thing, and could not see very well. I had talked with them a couple of times before, and we had figured out that she was a second cousin to my Nonna on my Mama's side. Their children were all grown, with families of their own.

The Sarros asked me why I was so sad, sitting there with my little suitcase. I told them that I had to move because I had used too much water washing my Papa's and my brother's clothes once a week.

"My Papa is coming to get me," I told them. "I do not know where I am going to live."

"Come live with us," Mrs. Sarro told me in Italian. "It is just my husband and me. The only thing I need for you to do is to take me to church each Sunday, just take my hand and guide me."

They had a two bedroom flat. I do not know if it was because of snoring or whatever, but they slept in separate bedrooms. However, the flat also had a Murphy bed in the wall. It could be folded down each night, and folded back into wall each morning. That is where I could sleep.

My Papa came to get me, and I explained that the Sarros had said I could live with them.

"Papa, it is your decision," I told him.

"I think that is the best solution," he said.

I think my Papa was sad that I could not stay with him, that I had to live with all those different people. They were all nice to me, they were wonderful to me, but it was hard. I was very bashful. I worried about asking for another piece of bread, or eating too much cereal in the morning. The people I stayed with <u>never</u> made me feel bad, but I always worried. I felt like I needed to keep both my feet in one shoe, if you know what I mean. These people were taking care of me, and I did not want to overstep my boundaries. I knew I had a duty to help any way I could, by doing the dishes, watching the children, taking them for walks. Anything that needed doing, I did it if I could.

The Sarros had an old wringer-style washing machine; after the clothes were washed in a tub of water, you had to carefully feed each item through two moving rollers. This would wring out all the extra water, but you had to be real careful to not get your fingers, clothing, or anything else caught in the rollers. Wanting to help, I said I could do the laundry, but Mrs. Sarro was afraid I might hurt myself.

"Please, let me try," I told her.

She agreed, but she stayed close by while I did my first load of wash. And sure enough, as I fed the clothes through the wringer, a strand of my long, curly hair got caught in the rollers. Quickly, Mrs. Sarro reached over and shut off the washing machine, then helped me get my hair free.

"I knew I shouldn't have let you do that," Mrs. Sarro told me. But she was not mad. I was only 12 years old, so I just was not able to use that machine on my own. But I kept trying to do anything I could.

Then in 1954, my Mama and sister were able to come to the United States on Italian passports, and we were all able to live together. We became a family again.

Chapter 2

My Mama was born in Verbicaro, Italy in 1911. She was just six months old when her Mama died. Her Papa remarried and had a son. The second wife also died, so my Mama's Papa married again, and had five children with his third wife. My Mama and her two older brothers were all raised by their Mama's brother, Uncle Orlando. He and his wife had a son and three daughters, and they raised my Mama and her two brothers like they were their own kids.

Mama and Papa, Wedding Day, Dec. 12, 1936

Rose Rinaldi

When my Mama and Papa married in 1935, Uncle Orlando gave them a small house. One bedroom, one kitchen. But it was made of brick, and was humid inside. And like his Mama, my Papa suffered from emphysema. My Mama said, "We cannot stay here." So they sold it, and rented a little place nearby. Then the owners needed the place for their own children, and my parents found another little house to rent. My older brother was born there. But after awhile, the landlord needed the house and my parents had to move again.

One of my Papa's first cousins owned a two-story place in town that she was renting out. One of my Mama's first cousins was living downstairs with her husband and two sons, but the upstairs was empty. No one was living there, and it was unfinished – just a big open space with no separate rooms.

"It's empty," my Papa's cousin told my parents. "Stay there, and fix it up. You can stay as long as you want."

My parents put up a divider to create a bedroom. They installed a little brick oven in the kitchen area, and a bathroom outside on the balcony. They made it their home. That is where I was born, in 1940.

That was also the year that Italy entered World War II on the side of Nazi Germany. I do not remember much about the war, except that food was scarce at times, both during the war and afterward. Our town was fairly remote. There was no fighting near us most of the time, but sometimes we would hear gunshots during the night. My parents worried that the fighting might come closer, or that the Germans would come to town and take what little we had left. We had heard of that happening to other people.

"Maybe we should go," they would tell each other. "They might be coming. Maybe we should go."

One time the gunfire was especially loud, which meant the fighting was really close. So we packed up all our food, and spent a couple of nights outside, hiding in our vegetable garden. There were no street lights in our town, so it was really dark at night, and you could not see us in the garden. But the fighting never came near us, and we were safe.

In 1943 the Allies invaded Italy, and Mussolini was thrown out. I heard about the American soldiers, how they gave out candy bars and nylons, but I do not think I ever saw any. If I did, I do not remember.

Sometime in 1944 or 1945, my Mama gave birth to a little girl, named Carmela. She was a good child. We did not have a faucet in our house, so my Mama had to go to a central place in town to wash our clothes, get water, etc. While she was out, I would watch the baby for her. But when Carmela was about 18 months old, she got very sick, with severe diarrhea, and died.

It was a hard time for our family. We had the funeral mass in the church, and she was buried in the cemetery. As was traditional, our friends and neighbors brought us food every night – pasta, meat, some bread. For people who were already struggling to feed their own families, it must have been a stretch to feed others, but everyone did their part. The women would pack the food in a huge basket, and one of them would carry it on her head to our house. It was a beautiful tradition.

A little while later, the cousin who owned the place we were renting said she needed it for her daughter and we had to move. So we moved in with my Nonno, my Papa's Papa. He lived in a two-story home, with a loft. The bottom level was storage, with a place to keep animals, wine, grains, and things like that. The main living level had a kitchen, a bedroom, and a bathroom. Upstairs was the loft area. It is a little hard to understand, but my Nonno had already given everything he owned to his children, so he did not own his house. My Papa actually owned the kitchen. His younger brother, who lived with his family in a house owned by his wife, owned the bedroom. And their older brother owned the loft, which is where he lived with his wife and children. He eventually rebuilt the loft to make it a better living space.

My Nonno had been living on the main level, in the bedroom and kitchen. When we moved in, my Nonno put a small bed in the kitchen, and he slept there. The four of us – my Mama, my Papa, my brother, and me – slept in the bedroom. There was a little cot for my brother, and I slept in the bed with my Mama and Papa. We had a table, chairs, and a little bench that we sat on in the kitchen.

My Nonno's bed was in a corner of the kitchen, with a chest, and a couple of shelves. He had a pet chicken that stayed with him, and Nonno built the chicken a little nest on one of the shelves. The chicken would lay eggs, which my Nonno would cook and eat. Each day when my Nonno would go out to meet his friends, to talk and drink a little wine, the chicken would go with him. My Nonno was not a tall man, about five feet two inches or five feet three inches, with a huge moustache. He always wore a big hat, and walked with a cane. It was quite a sight to see Nonno's chicken following him down the street.

My Mama cooked for our family, but my Nonno cooked for himself. The chicken would make an egg and he would fry it, or he would make his own pasta and sauce. Whenever my Nonno made his food, my Mama would send my brother and me out to play, or she would close the door of the bedroom and we would play on the floor or on the bed. We gave Nonno his privacy. And he would do the same for us.

My family kept a pig downstairs for awhile, but then my Papa's brother who lived in the loft complained, and Nonno said

Both Feet in One Shoe

the brother and his wife could use the pig pen instead of us. But a pig was an important thing to own. It meant that soon we would have sausage, lard, prosciutto, and other meats. Not being able to use the downstairs pen was not going stop my Mama. She went to a rural festival to buy another pig, a tiny one. When young, you have to take care of pigs very carefully, like a little baby. So my Mama took newspapers and whatever else she had on hand, and made the pig a little nest on the floor in our kitchen, next to our bench. That way she could watch him and take care of him as he grew. So we had the baby piglet on one side of the kitchen, and my Nonno's chicken on the other. When the pig got big enough to be on his own, my Mama's aunt and uncle (the ones who raised her and her brothers) let her keep our pig in a little pen underneath their house.

My Grandfather, my Mama and my sister Carmel in 1954 in Italy

It was not a perfect solution because we had to cross a main street to get to their place, but it let my Mama raise her pig.

My Mama also owned two little pieces land that she had inherited from her family, but they were too far away to keep our pigs there. One place had a little vineyard on it, and my parents used the grapes to make a little wine for their own use. But the properties were not really large enough to do much with them, and they were too far away from Nonno's home for Mama to keep her pigs there. So we kept the pig at my Mama's aunt and uncle's house.

A relative had a piece of land near where we lived in Verbicaro, and wanted to sell it. My Mama said, "That would be a good place for me to grow more vegetables, and maybe build a little pen for some pigs."

My Mama could not afford the entire piece of land, so it was split in half. We got the left section, and another relative bought the right section. My Mama was delighted. We would receive packages from a distant uncle whom she never met. There would be clothes, mostly winter items for men and women, so my Mama sold many of them to one of the priests in Verbicaro. With that money she paid for our new piece of land.

She put in a beautiful garden, and built a small house for the pig. Then she bought more pigs, and moved them into their new home. We were still living with my Nonno, but now my Mama owned some land nearby, where she could raise pigs and grow vegetables to feed the family. That little piece of property was hers, and she could do what she wanted with it. No one could tell her that she could not use it, or that she had to move her pigs. Bit by bit, things were getting better for our family.

My baby sister was born in 1948, when I was 8 years old. My parents named her Carmela, in memory of the little girl we had lost. So now there were five of us sharing the bedroom: my parents, my brother, my baby sister, and me. There were a lot of us living in that house and it was not a fancy place, but back then if you had a roof over your head it did not matter what the place looked like as long as the family was together.

My Papa was a shoemaker. He made everything by hand, and he was very good. Back then, few people could afford to go into the city to buy shoes. My Papa was one of three or four shoemakers in Verbicaro, which was a town of about 9,000 people. He would make people new shoes for summer, new shoes for winter. But our family, we used to get our winter shoes during the summer and our summer shoes during the winter. Because the customers came first, and we came last. We had to wait for our new shoes, because our Papa needed to put food on the table.

And most of the time, that was how he was paid – with food or other items. In those days, in a village like Verbicaro, almost nobody paid cash. Maybe one or two people had a little money, but almost everybody else would pay with whatever they had. Maybe some grain, some corn, some figs. Perhaps a little wine or oil, maybe a little piece of meat. Potatoes, beans for the winter, things like that. Sort of trading. Maybe once in a great while you might get a little money, but mostly it was trading. It really was a way to put food on the table.

It was a simple life. We had no toys – no dolls, nothing. Neither did our friends. We would play games with sticks and our imagination. We used to play marbles with little round rocks that we found. We took the thorns off of prickly pears, and used the prickly pears to make little houses and dolls. We would make chairs using little pieces of wood. Anything that we found, we would come up with a way to turn it into a toy, to have a little fun.

Our school was near our home. I had lots of cousins, and we used to play together after school. My Mama always knew where we were, and I had to be home by a certain time. There were no street lights in town, so when it got dark, it got very dark very quickly. I was easily scared, and I did not like walking through the dark streets with the houses towering over me. So I always made sure I was home at the time Mama said I should be there.

As I said, food was scarce both during the war and after it ended. So the people of the town opened a small cafeteria, where the children could get lunch after school. It was not for everybody – you had to have a little pass so you could get something to eat. But I had a pass. That was the first time I saw cheddar cheese. They cut it into cubes, and gave each of us a little cube and a slice of bread, or a little pasta. Whatever they were able to serve us. And that was the first time I tasted cranberries. They cut the cranberries into cubes, the same size as the cheddar cheese. We would spread the cubes of cranberries on a slice of bread, like jam. For some reason, I still remember the cranberries and the cheddar cheese.

I saw the ocean just once when I was growing up. The Mediterranean was not far away, about a 45-minute walk from our town. One summer, my brother had surgery on his knee. The doctor told my parents it would be good if they could take my brother to the ocean for a couple of days, to recover near the salt water, hot sand, and clean ocean breezes. I was maybe six years old at the time. One of our cousins on my Mama's side had a horse and wagon that we used to carry my brother and our things to the seaside. There were two or three families who rented a place together, so there were maybe 15 to 20 people, walking or riding in the wagon with all our gear. We brought food and we all cooked together.

As I said, that was the first time I saw the ocean. I was afraid of it. My Mama would try to get me to go into the water, but I used to cry and say, "No, no, I do not want to go in."

"But it is good," my Mama would tell me. However, nothing she could say or do made me any less afraid. I would not go into the salt water. It was just too big and too strange for me.

One of my aunts and her family came and stayed with us for a couple of days, walking over from Verbicaro to our rented house. When it was time for them to leave, I told my Mama I wanted to go home with them. My family was not leaving yet, because they had paid the rent for several more days.

"Who will you stay with when you get back to Verbicaro?" my Mama asked me.

"I will stay with my godmother," I told her. My godmother was my Mama's first cousin, the one who lived downstairs from us before we moved in with Nonno. My godmother had two sons but no daughters, so she liked having me around, and spending time with me. We were very close. So I walked home with my aunt and uncle and my two cousins, and then I went to stay with my godmother until my family came home a few days later.

My godmother is the one who took me to see my first movie. There was a room in town, near City Hall, where they would show movies from time to time. The first one I saw was about the life of Christ. It was very dramatic, and I remember it clearly, as if I just saw it. I guess my godmother thought a movie about Christ would be good for her goddaughter to see.

Then in 1952, my parents learned the US immigration laws had changed, and my brother could get a US passport and move to the United States. It was a hard decision, but it was an opening, a chance for something better for our family. My Mama's first cousin, her husband, and their sons were already living in San Francisco, and they said Pietro could live with them. But it was a big step, sending him traveling to America on his own. He was 14 years old, almost 15. Finally, my parents decided it was the right thing to do. The hope was that once Pietro moved to San Francisco, we would all be able to follow him, and soon.

"It's a little sacrifice," my Mama said of the separation from her oldest son. "With the help of God, I am sure we are all going to do well."

Pietro took the train to Naples, sailed to New York, and took the train cross country to San Francisco. Working after school and on weekends, he was able to save a bit of money, and he sent a little home to our Mama.

Chapter 3

In 1953, the US immigration laws changed again. My Papa was now able to come to the United States with a US passport, and he could bring with him a son or daughter under 18 years old, also on a US passport. Again, my parents talked about what to do. This was another great opportunity, but it meant leaving my Mama and sister behind in Italy, without knowing when they might be able to join us. The plan was that they would come to San Francisco as soon as they could, but there was no knowing when that might be. The decision was made: my Papa and I would get our passports, and join Peter in San Francisco.

My uncle and cousin (my Mama's brother and his son) joined us on the train trip to Naples, where my Papa and I would board the ship that would take us to New York City. I carried a small suitcase; I remember it quite clearly. It is funny, but I cannot remember what was in it. Not much. I know I had a pair of socks and sandals, and I must have had a change of clothes. But even though my suitcase was not very big, it was not full, either.

My Papa carried his things in a small wooden crate. By this time, my brother was staying with Olga and her husband Gigu in

San Francisco, so my parents asked what we could bring them as a gift from Italy. Word came back that they wanted a prosciutto. Now, you were not allowed to bring salami or other meats into the United States from Italy. So my Papa put the prosciutto in the bottom of his wooden crate, and built a little platform on top of it – a false bottom, so the prosciutto was hidden from sight. The prosciutto made the trip just fine, and no one ever discovered that we were smuggling it into the United States.

When we got off the train in Naples, we had a little time before we had get on the boat. So my Papa, uncle, cousin, and I walked around Naples for a bit. I had never seen such a large city before. It was so different from our home town of Verbicaro.

"Is this the way it is in the United States?" I asked.

"Oh, the United States is at least four or five times bigger than this," my cousin told me.

We walked through a couple of stores, and I fell in love with a little pair of scissors. I begged my Papa to buy them for me. I do not know why I wanted them so much. Maybe I thought I could use them if I needed to mend something, or maybe I had a needle and thread in my suitcase, and wanted the scissors, too. I really cannot remember why, I just know I begged my Papa to buy them.

"At the moment, we cannot buy them," my Papa said. "But when we get to San Francisco, I will buy you a pair of scissors." I believed my father. I knew he would make good on his promise.

When we got on the ship, the *Vulcania*, my Papa slept in a men's dormitory on the bottom level, near the motors. My bed was two levels up, in a room with three or four Mamas traveling with their children. There were four sets of bunk beds in the room, making eight beds total. I know that I had a top bunk, because I was able to keep my small suitcase up there, next to the wall, where nobody could see it.

Unfortunately, I was seasick almost the entire twelve days it took to sail from Naples to New York City. I almost never got out of bed. My Papa would come check on me each morning, and bring me a little something to eat.

"Please get up," he would tell me.

"I can't. I just can't," I would say.

My Papa would bring me more food at lunch time, maybe a little piece of Panini with some lunch meat inside, and a little fruit. But I didn't eat hardly anything except for a bit of water. I was too seasick. However, I did not want to waste the food my Papa brought. I knew the lunch meat would spoil, so I took it out of the bread and gave it away. But I carefully took the bread and fruit, and put it in my little suitcase. I made sure the Panini bread was opened up, so it would dry out and not get moldy. I am not sure why I did that, but I know that in my family, bread was important, sort of holy. If you do not have bread and water, you don't have anything. So each day, I saved a little more bread and fruit in my tiny suitcase.

The only time that I got out of bed is when the ship docked in Lisbon, Portugal. My Papa had made friends with some people he ate with in the dining room, a couple from Naples who were in their 60s or 70s. He told them about me, and that I stayed in my room all the time. So they came down to see me.

"Come on, we are going ashore and we will show you beautiful things," they told me.

To be polite, I said yes, and my Papa and I went out with them to see Lisbon. As we walked around I thought, "Oh my gosh, where are we? Are we in heaven?" Because I had never seen anything like it.

I saw a big beautiful doll, and to my surprise it was black. When my baby sister was born her godmother sent her a baby doll, the first doll in our town. It was bald. But this doll in Lisbon was several feet tall, with beautiful black hair and skin. I asked my Papa, "Why do they make dolls black?" Because I had never seen a person with black skin.

That day in Lisbon was the first time I ate a meal on the ship, in the dining room. I will never forget it. I had split pea soup with rice. It was very good. And then we left port, and I was seasick again, all the way to New York City, which was even more overwhelming than Lisbon.

We sailed by the Statue of Liberty, and went through customs on Ellis Island. There were all these people, everywhere I looked. And we were all standing in long lines, like cattle. You had to make sure you knew your last name, because sometimes they would change it. And there was a section with a nurse and doctor, who were examining everyone as they went through the line. We knew that some people would not make it through, because they were not healthy. But I was not afraid, because I was with my Papa. He held my hand, and was very loving.

From there we boarded the train that would take us to California. It was a three day trip, and the bread and fruit I had in my suitcase came in handy. That was what we ate for the next three days. However, a couple of weeks before we made the trip, my Papa had a new denture made because he had bad teeth. And his new denture really hurt. So I would go in the bathroom and put a little water on the stale bread. Soaking it in water made it easier to eat. That fruit and bread lasted us all the way to California.

I met a woman in the bathroom who decided to throw out her nylons. I looked at her and thought why would she do that. She met my eyes and gave me a piece of gum. When I returned to my father, I told him about what happened. He looked at me and said, "Where we are going, it's a good place." Being cautious, he also told me to throw out the gum she had given me. I trusted my father.

The train dropped us off in Oakland, and we rode the ferry into San Francisco, where we met my brother, Peter.

My Papa and I had made it to San Francisco. We made it.

Chapter 4

As soon as he could, my Papa got a job at a shoe factory down on Market Street. The owners were Italian-Americans whose parents had come from Verbicaro. One of our relatives knew them, and told my Papa they might be hiring. They had about 10 men working for them, making shoes. But it wasn't like back in Italy where my Papa did everything by hand. In the factory, it was all was done by machine, and my Papa was not used to the machines. After only a few weeks on the job, he had an accident with the machine, and hurt his finger. The owners told my Papa to go home and recover. But then I guess they could not wait for him to get better, because they hired someone else, and my Papa lost his job.

Next my Papa found a job in a meat packing plant, but after a few weeks he got laid off from there, too. So he rented a shoeshine stand on Fourth Street between Market and Mission. It was a good location, with a lot of walk-in customers. My Papa was his own boss, and worked by himself. The stand had two or three chairs, so customers could sit and wait until he was available. Unfortunately, after a while the company that owned the stand wanted to build a huge store on the site, which meant the shoeshine stand would be torn down.

Mr. Sarro, who I lived with for awhile, had a shoeshine stand on the corner of Geneva and Mission, near a drug store. Mr. Sarro was ready to retire (in the late part of 1954), so my Papa moved to that shoeshine stand. He would go on to work at that shoeshine stand for more than 25 years, until he retired at age 75.

I started junior high in the fall of 1953. We were still waiting for my Mama and sister to join us in San Francisco. It had been 3 months since I saw my mother. I couldn't hear her voice during that time and I had to rely on letters. Since my mother could not write, her cousin would write the letters for her. I missed her so much. I always thought of the day when she would come to San Francisco. I couldn't wait.

In the meantime, I was living with Elvira and her family, on Vienna Street. Each morning I would walk to my cousin Carmela's house, and together we would walk to the corner of Mission and Alemany streets, to meet a boy named Joe. He came to the United States about the same time as us, but on his own, just like my brother Peter. Joe's mother had been born in the United States, so like me and Carmela, he was able to come here on a US passport. Joe was a distant cousin of Yolanda's family, and was living with one of his relatives. Joe would see us from his window, and come down to meet us.

Joe, Carmela, and I would take a city bus to school together, to Everett Junior High School on Church Street in the Mission district, between 16th and 17th. None of us spoke much English yet, because the people we lived with all spoke Italian. We decided it was up to us to figure out how to get to school, because we did not want to bother the people we were staying with. Each of us depended so much on them, and they were giving us a room and a bed, and food to eat. So we felt the three of us needed to figure out how to get to school on our own.

We practiced taking the Mission Street bus before school started. The bus was always full in the mornings, and sometimes it was hard to read the street signs to know where we should get off. We noticed that at about 14th Street or 15th Street there was a furniture store with a huge clock out front. That was our landmark. We agreed that after we passed the clock, we would pull the cord to stop the bus.

It worked. We made the trip a couple of times before school started, just to be sure we knew what we were doing. After school started, we always followed the same routine. Of course, it was not fool proof. Sometimes we got off a few blocks early, sometimes maybe a few blocks late, but we still made it to school on time. We used to argue about when to pull the chord. "Pull it now," one of us would say. "No wait, not yet, not yet," the others would answer. But we made it. We made it to school.

Each morning we went to home room first, and then we spent the rest of the day in a class learning English. There were two classes, really, next door to each other. And the students were from all over. They were Italian like us, but also German, Spanish, you name it. We all needed to learn English. There was a large group of us from Italy, both northern and southern Italians. Nice kids, both boys and girls. We all got along, and we used to help one another.

The teachers were wonderful, I will never forget them. Miss O'Brien, she was of German descent. Tall and slender. And Mrs. Burrell, she was of Italian descent, and spoke a little Italian. They were both so nice. They would bring all kinds of things into the classroom – spoons, dishes, glasses, whatever. They kept them in a little cupboard, and would bring them out and tell us what each thing was called in English. They would put the words on the blackboard, and we would write them down. Miss O'Brien wore a lot of makeup, and she would tell us the names of what she was using, her lipstick or whatever.

Life was settling into place for me, but my Mama and four-year-old sister were still in Italy, living with my Nonno, my Papa's Papa, in that same little house. I finished my first year at Everett Junior High in June 1954, and we had good news: the US immigration laws had changed once again. My Mama and sister were now allowed to join us in San Francisco. We had some money saved, and to get enough cash for the trip my Mama sold one of the pieces of property she still owned in Verbicaro, the little vineyard. That meant my Mama and my four-year-old sister were able to come to the United States. Unlike the rest of us, they traveled on Italian passports, because they did not qualify for US passports. But the important thing was that they could come here. Like us, they took a ship from Naples to New York City, but instead of the long train trip, they flew from New York to San Francisco.

I remember the day they arrived. That night my father, brother and I went to meet Mama and my sister at the San Francisco airport. We were all so excited. When Mama walked off the plane, she had a scarf around her head, her eyes were blistered, and she looked so slender. We think the salt air from the ship may have caused the blistering. My sister looked fine. We all ran to greet them. I remember holding Mama so tight, not wanting to let go. She smelled like Mama - I missed that so much. She kissed the ground and said, "Thank God we made it." Our family was together again.

And we were able to live together as a family once again. The young man who had been sharing the place on Valencia Street with my Papa and brother moved out, and my Mama, my little sister, and I moved in. It was so wonderful, to feel like I had a home and a family again. Of course, we were not on our own for long. After a few months, my oldest uncle came to San Francisco with one of his daughters. They stayed with us for awhile. We only had two bedrooms, but there was a little room in the front where my uncle and my brother slept. My parents were in one of the bedrooms, and my cousin, my sister, and I slept in the second bedroom.

And, of course, we had a lot of extended family nearby. Several of our first cousins, second cousins, and other relatives were living in San Francisco; as was traditional, we pretty much called all the adults aunt or uncle, no matter what the exact relationship was. We lived at 25th and Valencia. One aunt and her family lived on Edinburgh, and another lived on Russian Street. On Saturday or Sunday we would take the bus to visit them. I think the fare was only 15 cents then, but with five of us (my Papa, my Mama, my brother, my sister, and me) that added up, so sometimes we would save money by walking home. My Mama also had an uncle living on Bernard Street in North Beach. He had a large family, with lots of kids. To make ends meet, they rented out rooms to boarders so there were always lots of people at their place. Once in awhile we would go there on Sundays. And sometimes these relatives would come to visit us.

Whoever it was and wherever we met, we would talk and laugh and eat. Nothing fancy, but good food – pasta, a little meat, vegetables, or whatever. Maybe a roast, a few spare ribs, or even hot dogs. We did not care. It was food on the table. No steaks, nothing like that, but we always ate well, and enjoyed ourselves. The adults would drink a lot of coffee, and maybe the men would have a little whiskey in the coffee. To me, the important thing was the togetherness. Family. I loved it when they told us all the old stories.

And we had friends who lived nearby who owned a car, and their son drove. They would come over to our place for coffee on Saturday or Sunday, and then we would go for a drive. We would go see where they were building new houses, sometimes we would go to the zoo, and we would go to the cemetery, to visit the graves of our family members and friends, to remember them. We did not do this all the time, just now and then. But it was nice.

None of us had a lot, but we made do with what we had and shared what we could. My Mama was a good shopper, and she always made us a delicious meal. If she had an egg, bread, and salt, she would make something wonderful with it. My Mama shopped at all the Italian-owned stores on Mission Street, and everybody on Mission Street between 22nd and 25th knew my Mama. She would say, "Oh, tomorrow, I come with the money." And they would say, "That's fine, take what you need."

My Mama never had a bad word to say about people. She was always nice to everyone. Because when she was young she had to work and could not go to school in Italy, my Mama did not know how to read or write, but if she had known she would have been a good businesswoman. Very good. And she always gave us good advice.

"Don't worry," she said. "Work hard, it will pay off. **Sacrifice**."

Not sacrifice in the sense that you do not have food to eat, but save. My parents really taught us to work and save. And not just in words, but by what they did. As soon as my Mama got here, she began saving as much money as she could. If there was any way she could put a little money aside, she did it.

All together: Rose, Mama, Papa, Carmel, and Pete in 1954

"I have never had a house to myself," she said. "I want to buy my own home. I will clean toilets, wash floors. I will do anything."

My parents were determined to buy a house, and nothing was going to stop them. Our Papa worked long hours at his shoe shine stand, and Mama got a job down on Howard Street, in an Italian-owned food processing plant. It was a full-time job, working with artichokes, and she earned 50 cents an hour. And whenever they could, my parents would earn a bit of extra money. A friend of theirs worked nights at the airport, cleaning. He lived nearby and anytime he needed a little extra help, he would give my parents a ride to and from the airport so they could work for him – cleaning bathrooms, hallways, whatever needed doing. Sometimes my parents would work Saturday night, sometimes

Sunday night, sometimes both nights. Anything they could do to earn a little extra cash. And they saved every penny they could.

At the end of 1955 – about a year or so from when my Mama and sister first arrived in San Francisco – my parents were able to buy a building with two beautiful flats on Caselli Street in Upper Noe Valley. My brother helped a bit, I think. He worked hard selling newspapers, and saved as much as he could. It was not as hard to buy place in San Francisco then, because the prices weren't as crazy as they are now. They paid $17,000 for the two-flat building. They made a down payment, and signed a mortgage. It was a proud moment, when we moved in. My Mama was so happy. She brought a little holy water home from church, and she sprinkled our new home to bless it. After years of renting and living with relatives, my Mama had achieved her dream; she owned her own home.

There was a tenant in the downstairs flat, and we moved in upstairs. It was a nice place. We had a front room, a dining room, a nice kitchen, two bedrooms, a bathroom, a back porch, and a little room just off the back porch. There was a stove, and we bought a refrigerator from a friend who was moving. My parents took one bedroom, my sister and I slept in twin beds in the other bedroom, and my brother slept in the small room off the back porch. People gave us sheets and towels as housewarming gifts. They were generous. We had a television in the front room, for guests, and someone gave us a small TV that we put on the back porch, along with a small sofa and a couple of chairs, so we kids would not mess up the living room while watching television. My Mama liked everything to always be clean and neat, no matter what might happen, so she put plastic on the good furniture in the front room, to keep it nice.

Chapter 5

After two years at Everett Junior High, my friends and I moved on to Galileo High School, in the North Beach area. My brother Peter had graduated from Galileo the year before, and now I was there as a freshman. It was a big place, but it was a nice school. Many of the students were from all over the world, but a lot of my friends were Italian, like me. We all brought our lunches, and we would eat together at the front of the school, maybe 10 or 15 of us, both boys and girls. Making jokes. Saying what we felt. It was great, it was really great.

We went to home room each morning, then to different classrooms for courses like biology, algebra, English, sewing, cooking, or gym. Most of the high school teachers were pretty nice. They helped if you needed more studying after school, or whatever. They had a different approach back then, I think. Not as much homework as they do now. Sometimes they would give us time to start our homework, maybe 30 or 45 minutes before the bell rang for the end of the school day. A lot of the kids who lived in the North Beach area had jobs after school, either helping in the family business or earning a little money in a coffee shop or whatever, so they did not have a lot of time to do homework at home. I think the teachers knew that, and gave us all time to do homework during the school day.

For me, it was a long trip to and from high school, on several different bus lines. I think school started at 8:45 a.m., and to get there on time I would leave home about 7:30 or 7:45 a.m. The trip home could take even longer. So I could not work after school. But shortly after I started high school in my freshman year, my Mama told me, "Maybe you should get a little job someplace."

So I got a job in a beauty parlor owned by an Italian-American man. He had married a woman from from Verbicaro, our hometown. His beauty shop was on Union and Van Ness, and I worked there on Saturdays. He was very popular, and very busy. A German lady worked there also, doing hair, and his sister was at the front desk, making appointments and greeting customers. I would shampoo the customers' hair, and get everything ready when he was going to do a permanent wave. If they needed me, I worked there every Saturday through all four years of high school.

The place my parents had bought on Caselli Street had a sort of basement on the bottom, three steps down from the street level. There was a small back room where we stored things, and where my Papa had a sort of workroom so he could repair things that were broken, make wine, or just tinker around. The front room on that level was larger, with a window in front that provided nice light. My brother and I turned it into a little room for ourselves, where we could entertain. His friends and my friends, we would all get together in that little room.

I think my girlfriends and I did most of the decorating in that room, because we put up pictures of celebrities. There were photos of Elvis Presley just about everywhere you looked. Frankie Avalon.

Paul Anka. Bobby Darin. Jane Mansfield. Annette Funicello. A lot of pictures, to make it feel fun. We had a few chairs and a table. Our Papa had an old record player that he let us use, and we would play music, maybe dance a little bit. Usually girls dancing with girls and boys dancing with boys, because we were all just friends. When someone got a new record, they would bring it over and we would listen to it. Sometimes our friends would bring a pizza, some chips, maybe some peanuts, or whatever. And we would have fun. We would drink Cokes – no liquor, nothing like that. Because my Mama or my Papa would come down and check on us.

We were all pretty good kids. Many had come here from Italy the same way my brother, my cousins, and I did, on their own or with one parent or family member, leaving other family members behind. A few were lucky enough to have come here with both parents. However each of us got here, we all wanted to better ourselves, to take advantage of the sacrifices our families had made so that we could grow up in the United States.

We went to school dances now and then. My brother would take me. And once in a while my parents would allow me to go to the Saturday night dances at Fugazi Hall, in North Beach. They were open to anybody, but a lot of Italian boys and girls would be there. Some of them would come with their parents. Again, my brother would take me, or he would go with his friends and one of my girlfriends would pick me up and we would go together. But we only did that once in awhile, because going there meant I needed a new dress and shoes. To wear the same dress and the same shoes, that was a no-no. It did not have to be an expensive dress, but it had to be something new.

And some Fridays, I would meet my friend Gracie on Van Ness and Market and we would take the #47 bus to Galileo High

School. Sometime after school, we would walk down to North Beach with a couple of our girlfriends, some of them worked in coffee shops down there, and we would go say hi, have a cup of coffee, visit, and then we would each take a bus back home.

I went to my senior prom with a friend of my brother. They were trying to put a music group together, and my brother's friend had a good voice. And I liked him, so I asked him to the prom, and he said yes. We had dinner in North Beach with my friend Gracie and her boyfriend Sergio (who became her husband). After dinner, we went to the dance in a big auditorium, and then the four of us went to Gracie's house. Her parents were home, and we all talked and had dessert and coffee. The boys slept on the sofas, and Gracie and I slept in her room. In the morning Gracie's Mama gave us breakfast. We had a good time.

For graduation, my Mama got me a nice little dress with matching shoes and purse. The ceremony itself was in a large auditorium, and we all wore caps and gowns. My parents, brother, sister, and a few relatives were there, and afterward we went to our house and had cake and coffee. A family celebration. It was a good day. My parents had come to San Francisco to give their children a better start in life, and now my older brother and I had both graduated from high school.

Right after graduation, I registered with an employment agency down on Market Street, and they got me a job training to be a bank teller with Bank of America. I worked there a couple of months, but I felt uncomfortable the whole time. I am not into numbers, and handling the money made me uneasy. There were people there to help me, to show me what to do, but it just was not a good fit for me. So I went back to the employment agency and told them I wanted something else. I think it took about a week, and they found me a job in the copy room at Standard Oil. When I first started they were using the old mimeograph machines to make copies of everything, but not long after I started work they switched to the brand-new Xerox machines. I was one of the first people to learn how to use it. I worked in a small room with that big machine, making copies. It was fun. I loved it. People were very nice. They would come from all over the building to bring me the things they wanted copied. "I need 10 of these." "I need 2,200 of these." I would make the copies, and then I would call them up and tell them that their job was ready. In the room next to me, six or seven ladies worked collating everything. All day long they stood in line, putting everything together. At least I got to sit down now and then. But we all got along, and we would get together at lunchtime and talk. It was very nice.

Things were going well. I had graduated high school, and had found a good job, that I enjoyed. It was a much better job for me than when I was at the bank. Anything that I do, I need to be sure that I can do it, and I have to be able to do it well.

Chapter 6

When we were growing up in Italy, my brother's friend used to come to our house a lot. His name was Salvatore Rinaldi, but his family used to call him Turuccio, or sometimes Turo or Sal. He was one of twelve children, but six of them had passed at childbirth.

Maybe Sal liked being at our place because it was a little quieter, with fewer people. He and my brother played together all the time. They loved a game where they threw buttons against a wall, and my brother would come home with no buttons on his shirt. When Sal was a small boy at our house, my Mama would feed him, wash his face, wipe his runny nose, and just generally take care of him. My Mama had the patience of an angel, with everything and everyone. Even other people's kids. She would share anything she could spare.

Rose Rinaldi

Rose and Sal in 1960

So my brother, Sal, and I all grew up together. It was relatively small town, which meant we knew him and his family well. My Papa made their shoes for them, and they paid us what they could, sometime it was homemade wine, some homemade olive oil, or maybe some fresh honey. Whatever they had.

Sal's Papa, may he rest in peace, went back and forth to the United States several times over the years, but Sal's Mama never wanted to move here, so the family remained in Italy. Sal's Mama, may she rest in peace, had a brother living in San Francisco, and his daughter got married a couple of months before I left Italy to come to the United States. About a week before my trip, Sal's Mama asked my Mama if we could do her a favor, and bring her niece in San Francisco a tablecloth as a wedding gift.

"Of course," my Mama replied. It would be easy enough to add the tablecloth to the box my Papa was taking, the one with the false bottom hiding the prosciutto.

About two days before my Papa and I were due to leave, I went to Sal's house with my cousin, to pick up the tablecloth. We had a cup of coffee with his parents, and visited a bit. There was a water fountain near their place, and one of my aunts happened to be getting water for her home. Sal's Mama invited my aunt to enjoy a cup of coffee with us. I was 12 years old at the time, with very light-brown hair, almost blonde, and a freckled face. The freckles disappeared as I got older, thank God, but back them I was really freckled. People sometimes thought I was German. My brother, my sister, and my cousins all had dark hair and dark skin, but not me.

Sal's Mama was kind of quiet, but his Papa was very open and outgoing, and said what was on his mind.

"Are you coming back?" he asked me.

"Coming back?" I said. "I have not even left yet."

"Oh," he says. "Are you coming back to marry Turuccio?"

I did not know what to say. I was only 12 years old.

Then my aunt, may she rest in peace, looked up at the morning sky, and said thoughtfully, "Who knows. What God wants, it could be."

And that was it. I left Italy, and came to the United States, to San Francisco. I went to school, I graduated, I got a job, and I worked hard. I think I was kind of lucky. I had a lot of friends, and I had boyfriends — or, not boyfriends exactly but boys that I liked and they liked me. One boy, who worked with my brother, kind of had a crush on me. He asked me out, and took me to a restaurant in North Beach. I still remember the place, although it closed long ago. I kept thinking that this guy could not afford a big meal. So we ordered a huge sandwich and we split it, with a little bit of salad or whatever.

And there was another boy, who was another friend of my brother. This boy liked me a lot, too. We were kind of like boyfriend and girlfriend, only I did not go out alone with him, I would go out with my brother and this boy would be there too. Then one time he tried to kiss me. He liked wine, and I could smell the wine on him. I thought, "Forget it. No way. This is not for me."

Then, while I was working at Standard Oil, Sal's aunt and uncle were getting ready to make a trip back to Verbicaro for a nice long visit. My family and I went over to their house to wish them a good journey. I was 18 years old. I do not know if Sal's parents had written to them or something, but Sal's uncle turned to me and said, "Why don't you come with us?"

"For what?" I asked, startled.

"Why don't you come with us and marry Turuccio?"

My first thought was no, no, no. I had good friends, I had a good job. I was not interested.

"No, I cannot, I am working," I told him politely.

So they went without me. And when they came back, they brought photos with them. Including one of Sal. They also brought a little gift for our family, I do not remember exactly what. So my Papa, my Mama, my younger sister, and I went over to get it, and to visit. They showed me Sal's picture, of course. And it was like lightning. I think it was meant to be. He was wearing a white suit, and he had really nice hair. I do not tell him this very often, but he is very handsome. I thought he could have been a movie star.

"Oh, yeah," I said casually. "He is kind of good looking."

Equally casually, I asked, "Is he engaged?"

"No, no, he is not engaged, but he has many girls following him," his aunt told me.

We had a little more coffee, chatted some more, talked about their trip, and then my family walked home. My Papa and sister went up to our flat first. As my Mama and I climbed the stairs, she asked me, "Eh, what do you think?"

"What do I think about what, Ma?"

"Turuccio is good looking, isn't he?"

Now, two years before, one of my cousins went back to Italy by herself to get married. Another cousin did the same thing a year later. And some relatives had approached me earlier, about going back to Italy to marry their nephew or cousin, or some sort of male relative. And each time I said no way. There had been a few other family members or friends who casually mentioned a young man to see if I might be interested in going to Italy to get married, and my response was always, no, no, no. No way. One time, one of my cousins came over on a Sunday, and brought us a huge cake. I asked my Mama, "Why did she bring this to us?" Then my cousin started telling me about a young man in Italy. And I said no.

Now, my Mama was asking me about Sal.

"Let's go upstairs and talk," I told her. And we went upstairs to our flat, and sat down, just the two of us.

Sal and I had grown up together, in a small town where everyone knows everyone. You know the bad and you know the good. I knew Sal was a good guy, and I knew his parents were good people. And I liked what I felt when I looked at Sal's picture. So for the first time, I was seriously thinking about going back to Italy to get married.

"My two cousins went to Italy by themselves and got married. I am not the type to do that," I told my Mama. "I could not go by myself."

"If you want to go, I am coming with you," my Mama told me. "You are not going by yourself. If I have to, I will work day and night to save enough money."

But first, I wanted to be sure that Sal really was not seeing someone else.

"You know how it is in Italy," I said. "They go together for six, seven years or more without it being an engagement. Before I say yes, I have to make sure."

So I wrote to one of my cousins, Rina. She and I used to play together all the time when we were children, and I trusted her. I asked her if Sal was really free, or if he had given a girl his word or a little promise ring, or something. My cousin was happy to hear from me, and she wrote back to tell me that no, Sal was not serious about any girl in Italy. There were a lot of girls who would follow him to church, or come to the tailor shop where he worked, and even if they did not need water they would come past his family's house to use the nearby fountain. But Sal was not serious about any of them.

And in fact, Sal was still in touch with my brother. They wrote each other, and Sal would ask Peter how I was doing. Peter had sent him photos of me, including my high school graduation photo. Sal was also close with my Nonno, my grandfather that my family had lived with for many years. Sal would go visit him, and bring him a cigar. I even had a photo of Sal lighting a cigar for my Nonno.

Maybe six years before, when my aunt in Verbicaro looked at the sky and said that only God knows, she was right. It was destiny.

I wrote to Sal, letting him know I was interested. He wrote me back. Our letters back and forth were not really lovey-dovey. Mostly they were about the details, about when I could come to Italy and how long I could take off work, and how Sal would come to the United States after we were married. And my Mama started saving every penny she could, for our trip to Italy, and for my wedding to Sal.

I needed a wedding dress. A friend of ours worked in the maintenance department at The White House, a huge, beautiful department store on the corner of Sutter and Grant streets in San Francisco's Union Square. It was known for its wonderful customer service and the luxurious goods it imported from France.

"Don't worry," our friend told my Mama and me. "Come to the store, and see what you like. We will say that you are my godchild or something like that, and they will give you a discount."

My Mama and my aunt came with me, and our friend and his wife met us at the store. I tried on a couple of dresses, and then I tried on the one that I loved. It is very simple, but gorgeous. Long scoop sleeves, all in lace. A high neck with little buttons all the way down the back, and a long train, at least six or seven feet long. With several petticoats underneath, which was the style then. It was the most beautiful dress I had ever worn. I loved it. I just loved it. So did my Mama, my aunt, and our friends. It was my dress.

It cost $1,500. With the discount, it was about $800 or $900. In 1960, that was a lot of money. I had not been working at Standard Oil for very long, but I had saved a bit. And my parents came up with the rest. It was a major purchase.

"Don't worry," my Mama told me. "We will manage."

I still have my wedding dress. My sister-in-law got married in it. So did both of my daughters, although they made a few changes, and they did not wear petticoats underneath, making it look much more simple and less poufy. After each wedding, we had it carefully cleaned and stored in a special box, to keep it in good condition. I hope that someday my granddaughters will be married in that same dress, the one I chose to wear when I married Sal.

Taking my wedding dress with us, my Mama and I flew to Italy on June 17, 1960. On the plane, I felt lucky because I had my mother with me. It would have been great to have my father there too, but I was grateful for one parent to share this with me. We were both nervous flying. This was my first time on an airplane and since I knew how to speak English, this trip was not that difficult.

Sal and I got married on Thursday, July 28, 1960. I was 19 years old, about to turn 20, and Sal was 21, a few months shy of turning 22. It was great to be back in Italy and see my relatives especially my grandfather. It was the last time I would speak with him.

Our wedding day in Italy, 1960

Chapter 7

Sal and my cousin Urbano met us at the airport in Rome. When I saw Sal, I felt an immediate connection. I think it was mutual. We both liked what we saw. Of course, we were a little nervous. It's a marriage. You do not know if it is going to work. You are taking another person, for a lifetime. In marriage, you take a chance. It is like going gambling or playing cards. You do not know how it will work out. But thank God, neither of us were desperate. For both of us, this was what we wanted.

Sal and my cousin Urbano helped Ma and me take the train from Rome to Verbicaro, where Ma and I stayed with my Nonno. He was still sleeping on a bed in the kitchen, and Mama and I slept in our old bed in the bedroom. We visited all my aunts, uncles, and cousins, and we started getting ready for my wedding.

Sal's uncle was the head priest at the main church in our town, so it was arranged that he would conduct our wedding mass. A week before the wedding, Sal made an appointment for us at City Hall. My Mama and I met Sal and his parents at City Hall, and Sal and I signed all the formal marriage documents. Afterward, we went to Sal's home, and had some wine and a nice dinner. We spent the day with most of Sal's family—his two sisters, may they rest in peace, his brother, his nieces and nephews. They were all there. Then Mama and I went back to Nonno's house.

A week later, Sal and I were married in the church, at nine o'clock in the morning. It was a full Mass. The church had celebrated an annual religious festival just a few weeks earlier, and the lights and decorations were still up. It was beautiful, just beautiful.

My Nonno's house was at the top of a hill, and not very close to the church. So I got dressed at the home of my aunt and uncle who lived a little closer to the church. Once I was dressed, Sal came to meet me there, and our entire bridal party walked to the church together. Sal's brother Elio was the best man and my cousin Rina, the one I wrote to asking if Sal was free, was my maid of honor. There were also three girls and two boys in our bridal party, each one holding a cushion or a little bouquet of flowers, or whatever, and they walked in front of us on our way to the church. As we walked to the church, the children went first, followed by Sal and me, the best man and maid of honor, and the rest of the group. I did not carry flowers, because that was not the tradition in Italy back then. My Godmother had given me a rosary and a little white religious book. I decorated the book with netting and a ribbon and bow, and carried both it and the rosary.

When we came down the stairs from my aunt and uncle's house and walked to the church, there were people everywhere, on the street or watching from the balconies of their homes, and wishing us well. Plus, they were curious. Although I grew up in Verbicaro, I had been living in the United States for seven years, and they had never seen a wedding dress like mine.

The church was packed. The boys and girls walked down the aisle first, followed by the maid of honor and the best man, and then Sal and I walked down the aisle together. That was the tradition then.

It was a hot day, and it was beautiful before the ceremony. However, as soon as we got out of the church, it started raining, with lightning and thunder. Someone held an umbrella over me, and someone else held one over Sal as we walked to the nearby photo store to take our formal portrait. And when I got there, I could not find Sal for a bit. It was confusing, but then he showed up and we got the picture taken, both the two of us and with the full bridal party.

Our wedding reception was across the street from the church, at the home of one of my cousins. She had several large rooms, which is why we chose her place, because we had about 125 guests. We served homemade Italian cookies and pastries, and a three- or four-layer cake. I know it was beautiful, but I do not remember exactly how big the cake was. We also had both homemade and store-bought wine and alcohol.

It was traditional to have someone at the reception with a basket of colorful Jordan almonds. They would be thrown down on the ground, and the children would scoop them up. But it was raining and the ground was muddy, so I told my relatives not to throw the Jordan almonds on the ground. But whoever was holding the basket of almonds did it anyway, and the kids went after the candy, even in the rain. They just wiped the mud off and ate them anyway. I guess they did not want to miss that treat.

As the reception wound down, I changed into my traveling clothes. It was about 2 o'clock when we caught the train to Naples to start our honeymoon. It was a really hot day, and my choice of clothes was a mistake. I wore a two-piece suit, camel colored, very light, with a nice long skirt, a jacket, a blouse, and a hat. I looked really good, but it was so hot on the train. I was just dying from the heat. The trip to Naples took about two and a half, almost three hours, because the train stopped at a lot of small towns along the way. Sal's Mama had packed us some bread and prosciutto, to eat on the train, but that was a mistake, too. The prosciutto was really salty, and we did not have any water with us. We ate it because we were hungry, and we were terribly thirsty for the next few days. When we got to our hotel room that night in Naples, I was so thirsty I could not get to sleep. The faucet in our room only gave a little tiny drip of water, so poor Sal had to get up and go out and buy me a bottle of water so I could sleep. Both of us kept drinking a lot of water for the next few days.

Our honeymoon lasted about a week. We spent a few days in Naples, then went to Capri, and to Sorrento. I do not remember if we went to Rome. I do not think so. I don't think we could afford it. But it was a wonderful trip. Just wonderful. Then we went back to Verbicaro as man and wife. Sal and I stayed with his parents. They had sort of moved people around a bit, to give us a temporary space of our own, with a bedroom, bathroom, and kitchen. Nothing fancy, but it was nice. And we all ate our meals together, as a family, so I did not have to cook.

Unfortunately, I had to be back at work in mid-August, or I would lose my job at Standard Oil. And Sal could not come to the United States for several months, until all the paperwork was done. So I flew home with my Mama, and my new husband stayed in Italy.

"Behave yourself," I told him before I left.

"Behave yourself," Sal said back to me.

"Don't worry," I told him. "I will."

Chapter 8

It took almost four months, but finally all the immigration paperwork was completed. Sal was able to come to the United States by the end of the year. He spent Christmas with his family in Italy, and New Year's in San Francisco with me and my family. I met him at the airport with my parents, his uncle, and several of our family's cousins. I was so glad to see Sal.

I was still living with my parents, my brother, and my sister in one of the two flats on Caselli Street, and Sal simply moved in with all of us. Sal and I slept in the bedroom my younger sister and I had shared. We even kept the twin beds because we could not afford to get a new bed. We added a small bed in my parents' bedroom, and my sister moved into their room. My brother remained in his small room off the back porch. It was a tight fit, but as always we made it work, and made do with what we had.

Sal was able to find work right away. Back in Verbicaro, one of his relatives owned a tailor shop, and Sal started learning to sew when he was 9 or 10 years old. When he came to San Francisco, there was a huge Italian-owned tailor shop called Bloise on the corner of Fourth and Mission. About 40 to 50 tailors worked there.

Many of them – maybe as many as 20 – were from Verbicaro. So Sal got a job there. He did well. I do not tell him this often, but Sal is a great tailor. From scratch, not just mending or whatever. He can make men's suits, women's dresses, anything. His first job in San Francisco was at Bloise, but over the years he went on to work at Smith Clothing in Oakland, then he went with Ambercrombie and Finch, Bullock and Jones, George Armani. On his days off he worked for Young Men's Fancy on California, to make extra money. His last job before he retired was at Neiman Marcus. Sal worked hard, and did well at all of his jobs. Plus, he made suits for our son, and all the prom dresses for our daughters. Whatever our kids needed, we bought the material and Sal made it. He is very talented – but don't tell him I said that. He knows. He knows.

Anyway, when Sal first came here we lived with my parents, and we both worked. I made what I considered to be very good money in the copy room at Standard Oil; every two weeks I would bring home about $86 or $87. Sal made a bit less at first, maybe $80 every two weeks. But it all added up. Like my parents, we both worked hard and we saved as much as we could.

Some of my fondest memories are of cooking with my Mama. We made sausage together, cookies, Easter bread, biscuits, whatever we needed. Ma always had a garden where she could grow fresh vegetables. We would can tomatoes, and anything else that was ripe and ready. We hung peppers to dry them, then used them in sauces and other dishes. I remember that when my Mama worked at the food processing plant, she would bring home the artichokes that they could not sell, and make a nice artichoke frittata. She would use a few scallions, a little bit of garlic, and it would be delicious. The next day the leftover frittata would look like it was spoiled, because the Vitamin C in the artichokes would turn the frittata green, but it still tasted great and it was fine to eat. We ate well.

And in 1961, we got great news. I was pregnant.

Which meant our little flat would soon be even more crowded.

"Let's sell this place," my Mama said.

A good friend of ours was in real estate, and he told us about a beautiful six-unit building on 17th Street. It was brand new, and unfurnished. My parents had bought the two-flat building for $17,000 in 1955; in 1961 they sold it for about $26,000 or $27,000, giving them the down payment on the new building. It was a down payment on a new future for us. We were able to move in before the baby was born, and we celebrated Christmas 1961 in the new place. I am so grateful to my parents. They made so many sacrifices for us.

The building had three flats on the bottom level (numbers one to three), and three upstairs (numbers four to six). They were what was known as a "junior five" flat – two bedrooms, a living room, and a kitchen. There was also a bathroom with a tub. And it was all brand new, which was great. There were no dishwashers, but each unit had a garbage disposal, and the building had a whole house vacuum, so you just hooked a big hose up to the wall and it was easy to clean the rooms. My parents and younger sister moved into apartment number five. My brother Peter, my husband Sal, and I moved into apartment number four. My brother used our second bedroom during this time.

As soon as they could, my parents rented out the other flats. This was not an easy thing to do, however, because back then it was standard for an apartment like that to be furnished. I do not mean things like linens or dishes, but people expected the landlord to provide beds, and a sofa, maybe a small kitchen table. We did not have any extra money, so it was a struggle to get each place ready to rent. We needed at least four twin beds, two for each bedroom. (We did not know if the people sleeping in the bedroom would be a married couple or their children, so everyone got twins.) We also needed a table and chairs, and some sort of sofa. That was the most we could do. Obviously, we did not buy the best furniture. We would furnish one apartment with the basics, rent it out, and then start working on finding furniture for the next one. Back then, there were not a lot of big discount furniture stores, so it was hard to find bargains. When my Mama walked to church or went shopping, she would watch to see if anyone had put a chair or something in the garbage. Whatever she found, we would clean it and fix it up, and use it in one of the flats. One by one, we got all the flats furnished and rented. Our first tenant was a man and his wife, and I think they paid $175 a month.

Of course, my Mama immediately started putting in a lovely garden. Vegetables. Fruit trees. Peaches, plums, prickly pears, you name it. Everything she could, she would grow there. And we all pitched in to take care of the place. My husband and my brother unclogged toilets, painted rooms when people moved in or out. All of the flats had Venetian blinds, and if one of them broke, my Papa would fix them. I remember seeing him sitting outside, mending them. He got really great at it. And we would wash the blinds from time to time. We would take them all down, and lay them down outside. We would take a big bucket of soapy water, and scrub all the blinds, then hang them up on the balcony to dry. Whatever needed doing, we did it. There were times when my husband, my brother, and I would be working until 1 or 2 in the morning to clean and paint one of the flats after people moved out.

I worked at Standard Oil right up until the birth of our daughter, Maria Teresa, on Jan. 26, 1962. Sal and I set up a crib in our bedroom, and the baby slept with us. My Mama was still working full time in a food processing plant. She told me, "You make more money than I do. I will quit my job and watch the baby for you so you can work." We lived next door to my parents, so it was easy for my Mama to care for Maria Teresa. We just left the playpen set up in our living room, and my Mama would come to our place to care for our baby. And if my Mama needed something from her own flat, it was quick and easy to pop back and forth.

Becoming a mother was like winning the lottery. I was fortunate to have my mother's help, advice, and direction on how to raise our first child. She was the best mother, teacher, and friend I could have asked for.

One time, Maria Teresa was asleep in the play pen in our living room, and my Mama dashed over to her apartment to get something. Somehow she locked the door behind her, with the key and the baby still in our living room. By the time my Mama realized she was locked out, the baby was awake, and crying because she was all alone. My Mama panicked. She did not call me, she called my brother Peter instead. Peter and a partner owned a nearby grocery store, and Peter was able to rush home and let our Mama into our flat. And everything was fine. They told me about it when I got home.

I became pregnant again soon after and our son Ciriaco – who we called Chuck or Charlie -- was born Jan. 17, 1963. After he was born my Mama said she would take care of both of my children but I said no. "You cannot deal with two kids." So she went back to work, and I stayed home.

My brother was still living with us, so both babies slept in a crib in our bedroom with Sal and me. Our babies were slightly less than a year apart. It was like having twins. Lots of bottles and formula, and about 12 dozen cloth diapers to wash. There was a washer and dryer in the building, but I had to go downstairs to use them. There were no disposable diapers back then. I had to wash them all myself. It was a lot of work.

When our son Charlie was about nine months old, my brother Peter got married. He and his wife moved into one of the downstairs flats, which meant Sal and I could move our babies into our second bedroom. It was wonderful to have our bedroom all to ourselves again. My parents and my younger sister Carmela (who was still in school) were still living in the flat next to Sal and me. With my brother and his wife downstairs, we each had our own place but we were all in the same building, and could help each other whenever it was needed.

Things were going well for all of us. Buying the six-unit building on 17th Street had been a good move. My brother, his wife, Sal, and I, along with my parents owned the building. Sal's work as a tailor kept him working all the time, six and sometimes seven days a week, and I took care of our home and the kids. We did not have a car for a long time, so we rode the bus. Sal would carry one of the kids, and I would carry the other. We had a stroller, but back then there were very few strollers that would carry two kids at the same time. At least I never saw one, and our stroller would only hold one child. So we would carry the kids instead.

The years passed happily and quickly. Then in 1969, I found out I was pregnant again. Our youngest daughter, Stefania, was born June 16, 1970. Our son Charlie was seven years old, and

Marie Teresa was eight. Sometimes Stefania teases me and asks if she was a "mistake," but I just laugh and tell her my body wanted a rest after having two babies less than 12 months apart.

But when we knew we had our third child on the way, we decided we could not stay in the two-bedroom flat in my parents' building on 17th Street. It was too small for a family of five. We needed more space. By this time, my brother Peter and his wife Shari had a son, Joe, and were planning to have more kids. So we started looking around, and found a two-story building on Saturn, about a block and a half from my parents' place. There were two identical apartments, on two floors each, and both with three bedrooms and two bathrooms. My brother Peter, his wife Shari, Sal, and I bought the place together. Peter, Shari, and little Joe moved into the upper unit, and Sal, Maria, Charlie, and I took the downstairs place. There was one set of stairs up to our place, and another set of stairs to my brother's place. We shared the washer-dryer in the garage. By the time Stefania was born in 1970, we had moved into our new home on Saturn. Things were going well, and the years passed quickly.

Chapter 9

Once Stefania was old enough, we did a lot of camping with our kids. That was our family vacation, because it was a cheap way for us all to travel. And I enjoyed it. Well, maybe the first time I did not because I hate bugs and dirt, but I got used to it, and learned to enjoy it. Sal and I bought a Coleman tent at a garage sale for $50. I was beautiful, with windows and a door with a net. We slept on air mattresses. And we had a little stove, and a cooler. We would bring all of our food with us, except for a few things we would buy fresh in the area. We would usually camp for five to seven days, and often extended friends and family members would join us.

A favorite place was Collins Lake, toward Woodland, up Highway 113, on the other side of Chico. It is such a beautiful area, with a beautiful lake. We got to know the owners, a husband and wife, and their daughter and her husband. They were Italian Americans. One time when we were camping there with a couple of our friends, we invited the family to have dinner with us. They came, and they brought five gallons of ice cream for dessert. The kids loved it. We all had a great time.

One time we went to a different lake, with a couple of other families. For some reason, that year the lake was dry. So the kids all teased their parents, telling us, "Oh, you brought us camping at a dry lake." They could not go in the water. But the campground was a nice place, with beautiful bathrooms and a place to wash your clothes, and I think it had a swimming pool.

We took other trips, too. A couple of years we went down to Santa Cruz. We took my parents with us, and rented a bungalow. My father loved the water and sand. For some reason, his legs started to swell. We had to call our doctor and his advice was no sand and no water for Papa. He had to take some medication for it. Not the news he wanted to hear but we had a good trip regardless.

Years later, when Maria and Charlie were about 10 and 9 years old, and Stefania was just a toddler, we went to Disneyland for the first time. One of my nieces, Ninetta, came over from Italy, and we all took Amtrak from Oakland. All six of us stayed together in a small room in a motel in Anaheim. It was crowded, but we had a great time. We loved Disneyland. We had never seen anything like it.

Sal and I took the kids back to Disneyland three or four years later. We had our first Oldsmobile station wagon, and we drove down and back with the three kids. Coming home from Disneyland, we wanted to see Hearst Castle. But we took a wrong turn. By the time we got to Hearst Castle it was 7 or 8 at night. Hearst Castle was closed, so we drove up Highway 1 in the dark. On that stretch of the coast, Highway 1 is just two lanes wide, and hugs the cliffs. It was scary. And then there were several motorcycles behind us, unable to pass on the narrow road. I was afraid, and told Sal to lock all the doors. In my mind I was thinking so many things about what might happen. I wondered if they might have a gun, or knives. And out comes my rosary, and I am praying as Sal drives along the highway. Finally, Sal pulled over and stopped, and the motorcycles waved "thank you" and went past us. And that was it. They were very nice. We did not get home until 11:30 or 12 o'clock in the morning. And we never saw Hearst Castle. But we had a good time.

We lived in the place on Saturn Street for about six years. Eventually, my brother Peter and his wife Shari decided they wanted a bigger house. By this time, they had three children – Joe, Eric, and Nina. So they bought a single-family home, and rented out their upstairs unit on Saturn Street. I tried to get my parents to move in there, but it had a long, steep stairway. Our Papa had asthma, and did not want to live upstairs. So they said no, and stayed in their place on 17th Street. I did not like the idea of strangers living above us, so Sal and I decided it was time for us to move as well. In 1976 we bought a single-family home in Diamond

My family: Maria Theresa, Rose, Ciriaco, Sal, Stefania

Heights. We still live there.

My Papa passed away on July 17, 1985. He had always had problems with his lungs, and was a heavy smoker. And when he made shoes in Italy, he worked around a lot of chemicals. It was not a good combination, and by the end of his life he was in and out of the hospital every couple of years. He died at home, in his own bed, with all of his family around him. He had a good life. There were hard times, but it was a good life.

After our Papa died, our Mama stayed with my sister Carmela for several months, but eventually Mama moved back into her flat on 17th Street. We tried to talk her into selling the place and buying a smaller home near my sister, my brother, and me, but she said no. "This is my home," she told us. She had several nice tenants who looked out for her, and she had her beautiful garden, which she loved. Every morning Ma got up and walked to church for 8 o'clock mass, then came home and had a nice cup of coffee. She had a routine, knew her neighbors, and was happy there. So we did our best to help her take care of things, to keep the place looking nice. Of course, she did a lot by herself. She would start at the top of the building and work her way down, sweeping and cleaning as she went.

She also spent a lot of time working in her garden. She loved it there. Many times she told us, "I hope I die when I am in this yard, doing something outdoors." On Nov. 8, 1999, she was out working in her yard. I had talked to her on the phone the night before, and we had agreed that the next day she would come over and help me bake cookies. I was preparing the dough when I got a phone call from the son of a friend of mine. He had seen the ambulance at my Mama's place, and told me he would come over and get me, and give me a ride.

My Mama had been working in the yard when she suddenly sat down on a step. Someone in the building saw her sitting there, came to check on her, and called 9-1-1. The ambulance came quickly, and they laid her out on the cement, trying to revive her. She was gone. Her heart just gave out. My Papa had suffered in his last days, but my Mama went quickly, while she was working in her beloved garden. I thought to myself, "Ma, you got your wish."

I think Sal felt it just as much as I did when my parents died. Sal was sort of their second son, I think because they knew him when he was a little boy in Italy. We lived with my parents when we were first married, and lived near them all of our married life. Sal and my Mama were especially close. Like I said, she used to wipe his runny nose for him when he was a boy. And Sal was comfortable with both my parents, and patient with them. We were all family.

After my mother passed, I felt so lost. My mother and best friend were gone. I missed her advice, our talks about her life, her laugh. It was hard to hear all those stories of her sacrifice, but I felt her pain and understood it. I knew she would always be there with me. I visited her gravesite at least once a week and stayed and just talked with my parents. It was my way of connecting with them again and it felt right.

We kept the 17th Street building for a year or two, but it was lot of work to keep the place as nice as my Mama always did. Sal and my brother Peter handled the renters, cleaning the places when someone moved out, and finding new tenants. But not all the tenants were easy to work with, and people would move in and move out. And both my husband and brother were working long hours, so I tried to do as much as I could myself. One day, I was watering the yard on 17th Street. Struggling with the hose, I slipped on the outdoor stairs, and fell down six or seven steps. I was sore, but I was not badly hurt. I was lucky I was not seriously injured.

"I can't do this anymore," I told Sal. "Let's sell the place."

It was a beautiful place, filled with family memories. It made me sad to let it go, but we just could not keep it any longer.

Today, our three kids are all grown, and have children of their own. All three of our kids graduated from college. All three got married in St. Vincent de Paul Church on Green Street in San Francisco. Maria and Charlie had their wedding receptions in the San Francisco Hilton, where my sister worked, and Stefania's reception was at the Westin San Francisco Airport in Burlingame.

Sal retired in 2005, but he still has a lot to do. Back in the late 1980s, Maria's husband John started working part-time as an usher for the 49ers football team. Soon, Sal started working as an usher, too. Eventually John's son Johnny and my son Charlie and his son Michael worked there also. So it is a family thing. When they started, it was at Candlestick Park. Now Sal and John still usher for the 49ers, but at Levi's Stadium in Santa Clara. Sal works the games, and an occasional concert or private party. He likes people, so he likes being an usher. After Sal retired he was able to work there a bit more often. He ushered at the Super Bowl 50 game in February 2016, and he is thinking he will probably stop in the next two years. I think it is time. It is a long drive to the stadium in Santa Clara. Sal has been riding back and forth to work with a young man who is a friend of our son, but Sal has ushered for 27 years, and it is time to move on.

About 25 years ago, we bought a second home in the town of Sonoma, up north in the Wine Country. We had friends and family there for decades, and now our daughter Stefania and her family live in Sonoma. We spend a couple days a week in Sonoma, and the rest of the time we stay in our home in Diamond Heights in San Francisco. We spend a little more time in Sonoma in the summer, because we like to take care of our yard. We have a little vineyard in one corner, and make our own wine. We planted several fruit trees, and every summer we have a nice garden, with lots of vegetables.

Life is good. We cannot complain. We stay pretty busy taking care of our San Francisco and Sonoma homes. Every fall I dry peppers and can tomatoes. Sal still sews when he has the time. We keep busy, because otherwise we would go crazy. Of course, in the back of our minds we are always thinking about how to save every penny. That is just natural for us. Once you go through all that we went through, it is just second nature to save as much as we can. I am sure there are a lot of people like us. When you come from the Old Country, and go through what we all went through, it does not matter if you are from Italy or Puerto Rico or Nicaragua or whatever. You never stop watching what you spend. We spend a little money here and there, and we enjoy it, but we still try to save.

For my 75th birthday in August 2015, our whole family went out to dinner. My oldest granddaughter Monica was traveling for her job and could not make it, but everyone else was there. It was nice. In my mind I do not feel 75 years old. But I have too many little aches and pains to fool myself. I am 75 years old. Still, life is good.

I do worry a lot, but that is just what I do. And I have had a good life. It was not easy to come to America when I was 12 years old, but it was worth it. My brother Peter and my sister Carmela both did well. And Sal and I are doing well. We own homes in San Francisco and Sonoma, a rental unit in Sonoma, and a four-unit rental property that we own with my sister in San

Francisco. Most important of all, Sal and I have a beautiful family. Three wonderful children, two great sons-in-law, one marvelous daughter-in-law, and eight amazing grandchildren and one little angel in heaven. Look at all that America has given us. We have enough, we have more than enough. It is true that I suffered at times. My parents suffered at times. But look at all my parents gave us, and what we were able to give our children, and grandchildren. It was worth it.

Rose's Easter bread, April 2005

Family Tree

Grandparents:
Pietro (Peter) Fazio married Carmela Cava
    CHILDREN: Francesco, Giuseppe, Vincenzo, and Salvatore

Parents:
Maria Angelina Lofrano Fazio and Giuseppe Fazio
    CHILDREN: Pietro, Rose, Carmel

Rose Fazio married Salvatore Rinaldi
    Maria Teresa married John Coito Vincent III
        Children: Monica Anne
                          John Coito IV
    Ciriaco ("Charlie") married Marie Borrecco
        Children: Jessica Marie
                          Michael Salvatore
                          Juliana Mia
                          Anthony Ciriaco ✝
    Stefania married Marc Girish
        Children: Gabriella (Gigi) Nicole
                          Dominic Angelo
                          Vincenzo Mario

Brother of Rose: Peter married Shari Erickson
                        Joseph
                        Eric
                        Nina
Sister of Rose: Carmel married Thomas Gouveia
                        Christine

My family today: (Left to Right)
Vincent Family: John, Maria, John and Monica
Rinaldi Family: Marie, Michael, Juliana, Jessica and Chuck
Girish Family: Stefania, Marc, Gigi, Vinny and Dom
Pictured on bottom: Rose and Sal Rinaldi

Made in the USA
San Bernardino, CA
27 January 2017